WALKING IN THE DUST: A DEVOTIONAL COMPANION TO DUSTPRINTS OF THE RABBI

A 14-WEEK JOURNEY OF SURRENDER, DISCIPLESHIP, AND COVENANT OBEDIENCE

A COVENANT PATH™ SERIES DEVOTIONAL
BOOK 1.1

RICH VAN DOORN

To every heart longing to follow Jesus more closely—
may your feet find His path,
and may His dust cling to your soul.

And to my family—especially Mary—
your love and faith walk with me every step.

FOREWORD

Discipleship was never meant to be a theory.

In the first-century world of Jesus, to follow a rabbi meant you reoriented your entire life around his presence, his teaching, and his way. You didn't just agree with what he said —you patterned your steps after his. You rose when he rose. You walked where he walked. You listened. You watched. You followed.

That kind of discipleship leaves a mark.

The ancient Hebrew blessing, *"May you be covered in the dust of your Rabbi,"* wasn't poetic metaphor—it was the reality of those who walked closely enough to be changed by the journey. That's the heartbeat behind this devotional.

Walking in the Dust is not a collection of inspirational thoughts. It's a daily invitation to draw near. To slow down. To study the way of the Rabbi and shape your life around His voice. Each week explores a vital theme of discipleship, rooted in Scripture and enriched by the Jewish worldview that Jesus lived and taught in. You'll find Torah rhythms, Hebraic insights, personal reflection, and a call to visible obedience.

But most importantly—you'll find Jesus.

I pray that as you move through these 15 weeks, your faith deepens, your ears grow more attuned to His whisper, and your life begins to look more and more like the One you follow.

Because the goal is not just to know the Rabbi.
The goal is to become like Him.

Let's walk the path together.
—Rich Van Doorn

THE COVENANT PATH™ SERIES MAP

WALKING THE WAY OF THE RABBI — ONE BOOK, ONE STEP AT A TIME

Your Journey Has Begun...

This Devotional — *Walking in the Dust* — is just the next step in a 17-book discipleship journey.

Each book in *The Covenant Path ™* series is paired with:

- A **Core Book** – Theological and historical foundations
- A **Devotional** – Six-day spiritual practice + Sabbath reflection
- A **Leader Guide** – Cultural insights, Hebraic terms, and small group support

---

THE COVENANT PATH™ SERIES (CONFIRMED TITLES & SUBTITLES)

1. **Dustprints of the Rabbi**: *Discipleship in the Texture of Torah and Grace*

2. **Hear, O Israel**: *Living the Shema in a World of Competing Voices*

3. **Called to the Fire**: *Becoming a Holy People in a Culture of Blending*

4. **Kingdom Beyond the Jordan**: *The Mission of Jesus in the Places We Fear to Go*

5. **Crimson Covenant**: *From Passover to the Cross and the Blood That Bought Us*

6. **The Cup and the Cry**: *Gethsemane, Judgment, and the Obedience That Redeems*

7. **Streams Beneath the Sand**: *Finding Presence and Provision in Wilderness Seasons*

8. **Strong and Shattered**: *What Samson Taught Us About Misused Strength and Second Chances*

9. **Shade for the Scorched**: *Shelter in the Midday Heat of Life's Hardest Days*

10. **Rooted in the Wind**: *Resilience, Trust, and the Torah of the Desert*

11. **Psalms from the Edge**: *Songs of the Wilderness, Hope, and the Haunted Heart*

12. **Voice Like a Shofar**: *Calling Out to God in Praise, Protest, and Prophetic Hope*

13. **Every Line a Return**: *Praying Our Way Back to Covenant*

14. **When Thrones Collide**: *Living Allegiant to the King in a World of Caesar*

15. **Corinth Wasn't Ready**: *Confronting Compromise in the Church and the City*

16. **Dwelling Among Us**: *Becoming the Temple God Meant to Fill*

17. **The Exodus Still Echoes**: *How God's Rescue Story Keeps Repeating Through Us*

HOW TO KEEP WALKING

Each step includes:

- A teaching book
- A companion devotional
- A leader guide like this one

Start with the next title — or gather a new group to walk through this one again.

Discipleship is not a class. It's a path. The Rabbi is still walking. So must we.

INTRODUCTION

The dust still rises.

It rises from deserts and doorways, from mountain paths and city streets, from the quiet, surrendered footsteps of those who dared to follow the Rabbi — even when the road disappeared into shadows.

In Jesus' world, **dust was the mark of nearness**. To walk behind a Rabbi in the first century was not to attend a class or memorize a creed. It was to order your entire life around His steps — so closely that His dust would cling to you. And that, dear reader, is what this devotional is about.

THIS IS NOT A DEVOTIONAL FOR THE CASUAL READER

This is a companion guide for those who want to live differently — who long to walk the ancient road of discipleship, not just read about it. Each of the 14 weeks in this devotional corresponds to a chapter in *Dustprints of the Rabbi,* the first book in the 17-volume Covenant Path™ series. If that book cast the vision, this devotional is your **pathway for practice**.

WHAT YOU'LL ENCOUNTER

Each week contains six days of engagement (Monday–Saturday), followed by an optional Sabbath reflection for group or personal use.

You'll engage with:

- **Scripture passages** — not as boxes to check, but invitations to listen
- **Midrashic and Hebraic insights** — drawn from the world Jesus knew
- **Historical context and modern stories** — to root timeless truth in real life
- **Heart-level questions** — that call you not just to think, but to walk
- **Covenant obedience** — visible steps that turn belief into faithfulness

WHY DUST?

Because dust tells a story.

It speaks of nearness.

It reveals movement.

It shows that you didn't just admire the Rabbi — you walked so close behind Him that **your life was marked by His**.

We live in a world that prizes visibility, platform, and clarity. But the Kingdom treasures something quieter:

Faithful footsteps.
Dust-covered sandals.
Hearts so surrendered that they move before they understand.

YOUR ROLE IN THE JOURNEY

You are not expected to be perfect. But you are invited to be present. To return each day. To open your hands. To let the dust cling again. The Covenant Path is not about information. It is about transformation.

One step.
One prayer.
One act of obedience at a time.

LET'S BEGIN

The Rabbi still walks.
His dust still rises.
And the path still waits for those who are willing to come and see — and follow.
So take off your shoes.
Slow your heart.
Open this book.
And walk.

WEEK 1: DUST ON YOUR FEET

BASED ON CHAPTER 1 OF DUSTPRINTS OF THE RABBI

Focus Verse:

"Follow Me."

— *MATTHEW 4:19*

Theme: Trusting the Rabbi enough to walk behind Him before you understand the road.

Week Preview: Discipleship doesn't begin with understanding. It begins with movement. In the first century, students didn't ask for an explanation — they responded to a call. This week invites you into that same posture: following Jesus before you have all the answers. Dust was the proof of proximity in ancient Israel. And it still is today. When you walk behind the Rabbi, dust will cling to your soul. This week, we begin the journey not with certainty — but with trust.

DAY 1 — THE FIRST STEP

Scripture: *Luke 5:1–11*

Reflection: Peter didn't need a seminary degree to say yes. He didn't even need a plan. When Jesus stepped into his boat, the invitation wasn't wrapped in clarity — it was clothed in presence. The Rabbi called, and Peter dropped everything. That's how it begins. Following Jesus means leaving behind what feels familiar for a road that doesn't promise ease — but does promise Him.

Prompt:

- *Where is Jesus inviting you to follow Him without full clarity?*
- *What are you still clinging to that keeps your feet clean — but your heart distant?*

DAY 2 — A CALL WITHOUT A MAP

Scripture Readings:

- *Genesis 12:1–4* — Abraham's call
- *Matthew 4:18–22* — Peter and Andrew's call

Reflection: Abraham left his country without knowing the destination. Peter and Andrew left their nets without knowing the outcome. This is the rhythm of covenant trust. God calls. We move. Not because we understand, but because we believe the One who's leading is worth following.

Application Questions:

- *What part of your life have you asked Jesus to explain before you obey?*
- *How would your next step change if you trusted the Caller more than the call?*

DAY 3 — SITTING IN THE DUST

Mishnah Insight:

"Let your house be a meeting place for sages; sit in the dust of their feet and drink in their words with thirst."

— *PIRKEI AVOT* 1:4

Reflection: In the world of the Talmidim, dust was sacred. It told a story: "I have walked behind my teacher." To sit at a rabbi's feet was an act of surrender, not status. It meant listening so closely, the dust of his journey marked your own. Discipleship today is no different. It's not about what you know — it's about how closely you walk.

Prompt:

- *How "dusty" are your spiritual sandals?*
- *What practices help you stay close enough to hear His voice in everyday moments?*

DAY 4 — THE QUIET ROAD

Story:

A young woman left a career path that promised recognition. She stepped into a life of caregiving — unseen, unnoticed, uncelebrated. "No one claps for obedience," she said. "But I know the Rabbi sees." Discipleship isn't loud. It's faithful. It's marked by small yeses, by choosing presence over platform — dust over applause.

Challenge:

- *What step of obedience are you resisting because it feels too small?*
- *Who is watching your dustprints — even if they never say a word?*

DAY 5 — THE COVENANT MIRROR

Pause to reflect on these questions:

1. *When have I followed Jesus without knowing where it would lead?*
2. *What comforts keep me from stepping out in faith?*
3. *What habits make it easier for me to walk close to the Rabbi?*
4. *Am I more interested in direction or in presence?*
5. *What legacy of dust do I want my life to leave behind?*

Write what stands out. Sit with the silence. Let the Spirit speak.

DAY 6 — WALK IT OUT

Visible Challenge: Today, take one bold, visible step that reflects proximity to the Rabbi:

- Pray out loud in a place you've never dared.
- End a habit that distances you from Him.
- Begin a conversation or act of service that leaves a dustprint of obedience.

Prayer:

Jesus, I want to walk in Your dust. Not just with belief, but with motion. Call me again — and I will follow. Even when I don't understand, Let my life say "yes."

Amen.

OPTIONAL — SABBATH GATHERING / GROUP QUESTIONS

If you're meeting with others or taking Sabbath reflection time, use these:

1. *Where did you follow Jesus this week without having full understanding?*
2. *What was your "net" — and did you drop it?*
3. *How did dust mark your soul this week?*
4. *Where is He calling you next?*

WEEK 2: COME AND SEE

BASED ON CHAPTER 2 OF DUSTPRINTS OF THE RABBI

Focus Verse:

____

"Come and see."

— *JOHN 1:39*

____

Theme: Discipleship begins with a willingness to look closer — not with perfect faith, but with enough curiosity to take the next step.

Week Preview: Jesus doesn't demand full understanding before He invites you in. He simply says, *"Come and see."* In the ancient world, discipleship began with the eyes — with observation, curiosity, and presence. The journey began not with answers, but with the courage to draw near. This week invites you to look again — to step out of your assumptions, your spiritual apathy, or your safe distance, and follow Him closely enough to see who He really is.

DAY 1 — THE INVITATION

Scripture: *John 1:35–42*

Reflection: Andrew didn't have a theological argument. He had a moment. He heard a voice and followed. And when Jesus noticed him trailing behind, He didn't lecture. He simply said, *"What are you seeking?"* When Andrew asked where He was staying, Jesus responded with an open invitation: *"Come and see."* That's how discipleship begins — not with full understanding, but with a heart willing to walk closer.

Prompt:

- *What am I really seeking in my walk with Jesus right now?*
- *Am I willing to take the next step before all my questions are answered?*

DAY 2 — FROM CURIOSITY TO COVENANT

Scripture Readings:

- Exodus 3:1–6 — Moses and the burning bush
- John 1:43–51 — Philip and Nathanael

Reflection: Moses turned aside to look — and everything changed. Nathanael doubted until he looked — and Jesus met him in his honesty. God often reveals Himself to those who are willing to pause, turn, and look again. Some of the deepest covenant invitations begin with a simple glance toward what seems unfamiliar, even impossible.

Application Question:

- *What part of your life is God calling you to revisit with fresh eyes?*
- *Where is He asking you to come closer — even through your doubts?*

DAY 3 — THE DUST OF THE THRESHOLD

Mishnah Insight:

"He who welcomes a sage into his home is as if he has welcomed the Shekhinah."

— *AVOT DE-RABBI NATAN 11*

Reflection: In Jewish tradition, to welcome a rabbi was to welcome the presence of God. Andrew and the other disciple didn't ask for a sermon. They asked, *"Where are You staying?"* They wanted to see where Jesus *dwelt* — where His life happened, where His rhythms and presence resided. The first step in following Jesus is choosing to enter the doorway — the space where presence is found and transformation begins.

Prompt:

- *What space in your life have you kept off-limits to Jesus' presence?*
- *Are you welcoming Him into your daily rhythms — not just your theology?*

DAY 4 — THE RIPPLE EFFECT

Story:

Andrew didn't just follow Jesus. He ran and got Simon. Discipleship isn't a private revelation — it's a public invitation. When we truly *see* the Rabbi, we long for others to see Him too. It starts with a personal encounter, but it always leads to shared dust.

Challenge Questions:

- *Who in your life needs the same invitation Jesus gave you — "Come and see"?*
- *What holds you back from inviting others into what you've found?*

DAY 5 — THE COVENANT MIRROR

Reflect with honesty:

1. *Where have I responded to Jesus with apathy instead of movement?*
2. *What am I afraid I'll see if I come closer to Him?*
3. *Who in my life is waiting to be invited to "come and see"?*
4. *Have I settled for watching Jesus from a safe distance?*
5. *What would change if I walked across the threshold into deeper presence?*

Write what stands out. Sit in silence. Let the Spirit speak.

DAY 6 — WALK IT OUT

Visible Challenge: This week, open a literal or symbolic space for Jesus to dwell:

- Invite Him into your morning routine.
- Welcome Him into a relationship you've kept separate.
- Physically walk your neighborhood and pray, *"Jesus, help them see You."*

Prayer:

Rabbi Jesus, You don't force Yourself into my life — You invite me into Yours. Let me come closer. Let me see more clearly. And let others see You through me.

Amen.

OPTIONAL — SABBATH GATHERING / GROUP QUESTIONS

1. *How did you respond to the invitation to "come and see" this week?*
2. *What part of your life has become more open to Jesus?*
3. *Who did you share the invitation with — and what happened?*

WEEK 3: THE YOKE WE CARRY

BASED ON CHAPTER 3 OF DUSTPRINTS OF THE RABBI

Focus Verse:

"Take My yoke upon you and learn from Me, for I am gentle and humble in heart, and you will find rest for your souls."

— MATTHEW 11:29

Theme: Jesus invites us to carry not a burden of religion, but a rhythm of relationship. His yoke forms us, frees us, and reshapes how we walk through the world.

Week Preview: In the first-century world, every rabbi had a "yoke" — a unique way of interpreting and living out the Torah. To take on a rabbi's yoke was to submit your life to his teaching and walk so closely behind him that his dust marked your feet. Jesus' yoke isn't lighter because it's easier — it's lighter because He carries it with us. This week, you'll explore what it means to live under the yoke of Jesus, walking in His rhythm and surrendering to His way.

DAY 1 — AN INVITATION TO LEARN

Scripture: *Matthew 11:28–30*

Reflection: Jesus didn't offer rest by removing all responsibility — He offered rest through intimacy. "Take My yoke," He said. Not someone else's. Not the one religion tries to lay on your shoulders. His. His gentleness becomes your formation. His humility becomes your covering. His nearness becomes your rest.

Prompt:

- *What burdens are you carrying that Jesus never asked you to?*
- *What would rest look like if it came through walking closely with Him?*

DAY 2 — RHYTHM OVER STRIVING

Scripture Readings:

- Deuteronomy 6:4–9 — The Shema
- 1 John 5:3 — His commands are not burdensome

Reflection: The Shema was not just a prayer — it was a pattern. Morning, evening, walking, resting — the yoke of Torah formed every moment. Jesus didn't erase that rhythm — He embodied it. When love becomes the reason we obey, the yoke becomes light. It no longer crushes us. It shapes us.

Application Questions:

- *What daily rhythms shape your spiritual walk more than Scripture?*
- *How can love reframe the way you see obedience?*

DAY 3 — IN THE RABBI'S DUST

Mishnah Insight:

"Let your house be a meeting place for sages; sit in the dust of their feet and drink in their words with thirst."

— *PIRKEI AVOT* 1:4

Reflection: To walk so closely behind your rabbi that the dust of his sandals coated your clothes was a badge of honor. It meant you were close enough to learn, to imitate, to change. Jesus calls you to take His yoke — and in doing so, stay near enough that His dust shapes your daily life.

Prompt:

- *Are you walking close enough to Jesus to be formed by His rhythm?*
- *What would others see on you if they looked for the Rabbi's dust?*

DAY 4 — THE QUIET WEIGHT

Story:
A teacher once said,

"The most powerful lessons of Jesus weren't shouted — they were whispered between steps."

Many of the people who changed the world didn't carry microphones; they carried towels. They bore the weight of Jesus' yoke in homes, behind hospital curtains, in quiet faithfulness. That's where His gentleness shines brightest.

Challenge Questions:

- *Where might Jesus be calling you to serve quietly, without recognition?*
- *What kind of yoke would others say you carry — and how could that change?*

DAY 5 — THE COVENANT MIRROR

1. *What false yokes have you accepted — achievement, approval, control?*
2. *Where do you feel weighed down in your walk with Jesus?*
3. *What would happen if you truly believed Jesus is gentle and humble in heart?*
4. *How does rest show up in your life — if at all?*
5. *Are you learning from Jesus — or just working for Him?*

Write what stands out. Sit with the silence. Let the Spirit speak.

DAY 6 — WALK IT OUT

Visible Challenge: This week, trade one burden for a better rhythm. Choose one of the following — or create your own:

- Replace multitasking with 10 minutes of focused stillness.
- Begin or end your day with the words, "I walk in Your rhythm, not mine."
- Write out Matthew 11:28–30 and post it where you'll see it daily.

Prayer:

Rabbi Jesus, I've carried too much — and I've called it faith. Help me to walk in Your pace, learn from Your voice,
and live from a place of rest. Teach me to carry only what You give me. Let Your yoke be enough.
Amen.

OPTIONAL — SABBATH GATHERING / GROUP QUESTIONS

1. *What part of Jesus' yoke do you find hardest to receive?*
2. *How did your understanding of "rest" shift this week?*
3. *What false burden did you lay down — and how did that feel?*

WEEK 4: HONOR AND SHAME

BASED ON CHAPTER 4 OF DUSTPRINTS OF THE RABBI

Focus Verse:

"For the joy set before Him He endured the cross, scorning its shame, and sat down at the right hand of the throne of God."

— HEBREWS 12:2B

Theme: The path of discipleship doesn't avoid shame — it redeems it. Jesus bore public disgrace to restore our honor and reshape how we see ourselves and others.

Week Preview: In the world of Jesus, shame was not just a feeling — it was a public identity. Honor was everything, and losing it could mean exile from community, worship, and belonging. But Jesus redefined both. This week invites you to walk into places of personal shame and societal rejection with new eyes — eyes that see through the lens of covenant restoration. Jesus not only carried our shame — He transformed it into a new way of living.

DAY 1 — SCORNING THE SHAME

Scripture: *Hebrews 12:1–3*

Reflection: Jesus didn't just die for sin. He bore the full weight of public humiliation — spit, mockery, nakedness, betrayal. In doing so, He exposed the shallowness of the world's honor system and redefined glory on His own terms. The cross was not just pain. It was shame — transformed into triumph.

Prompt:

- *What shame still shapes how you see yourself?*
- *What would it mean to walk with the Rabbi through it instead of around it?*

DAY 2 — A WOMAN AT HIS FEET

Scripture Readings:

- *Luke 7:36–50*
- *Isaiah 61:7*

Reflection: She wept at His feet. Hair undone, tears mingling with perfume and dust. Every rule said she didn't belong. But Jesus redefined her value — not by status, but by love. In the kingdom of God, honor is not earned. It's restored by grace.

Application Questions:

- *Where have you believed your shame disqualifies you from closeness with Jesus?*
- *What does this story teach you about how He sees you?*

DAY 3 — SHAME AND THE COMMUNITY

Mishnah Insight:

"He who humiliates his neighbor in public has no share in the world to come"

— *BAVA METZIA 59A*

Reflection: n Jewish culture, shame was social currency. To humiliate someone was a serious offense. Jesus not only protected the shamed — He ate with them. Honored them. He redefined discipleship as restoring the honor of others, not protecting your own.He stood.

Prompt:

- *How do you respond when others are shamed — online or in real life?*
- *Who in your life needs to be restored with honor?*

DAY 4 — SHAME IN THE MIRROR

Story:
A man once said,

"I didn't doubt Jesus could forgive me — I doubted He wanted to.'

Shame lingers when we confuse God's mercy with human rejection. But the cross wasn't just about removing sin. It was about restoring dignity. In Christ, we are not just cleaned — we are clothed.

Challenge Questions:

- *What shame are you still trying to hide instead of heal?*
- *Where is Jesus offering you a robe of honor, and are you willing to receive it?* ·

DAY 5 — THE COVENANT MIRROR

Reflect deeply:

1. *What moments in my life still carry the sting of shame?*
2. *How have I treated others through the lens of performance instead of grace?*
3. *Where do I fear being exposed or misunderstood?*
4. *How does the cross of Jesus change my response to failure — mine or others'?*
5. *What would it look like to be someone who restores honor this week?*

Write what stands out. Sit with the silence. Let the Spirit speak.

DAY 6 — WALK IT OUT

Visible Challenge: Restore honor this week — for yourself or someone else:

- Speak truth over someone who doubts their worth.
- Confess something quietly to Jesus that shame has kept hidden.
- Write a letter of blessing to someone who feels unseen.

Prayer:

Rabbi Jesus, You bore my shame so I wouldn't have to wear it. Clothe me with grace. Teach me to honor others the way You honored the broken. Help me walk in the dignity You died to restore.

Amen.

OPTIONAL — SABBATH GATHERING / GROUP QUESTIONS

1. *How has shame affected your spiritual journey?*
2. *Where have you seen Jesus restore your dignity or someone else's?*
3. *What practical way can you walk in restored honor this week?*

WEEK 5: SITTING AT HIS FEET

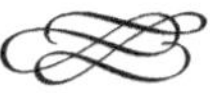

BASED ON CHAPTER 5 OF DUSTPRINTS OF THE RABBI

Focus Verse:

"Mary...sat at the Lord's feet listening to what He said."

— LUKE 10:39

Theme: Discipleship begins not with doing, but with being — resting in the presence of the Rabbi, not rushing to earn it.

Week Preview: In a world that worships busyness, Jesus honors stillness. Mary of Bethany chose something radical: she stopped. She sat. She listened. In first-century Jewish culture, to sit at a rabbi's feet was not simply to relax — it was to declare, "I am Your disciple." This week is an invitation to break from the tyranny of performance and come back to the sacred posture of presence. Sit. Listen. Let the dust of the Rabbi settle on your soul.

DAY 1 — CHOOSING THE BETTER PART

Scripture: *Luke 10:38–42*

Reflection: Martha welcomed Jesus. Mary worshiped Him. Both women served — but only one stopped long enough to be served by His words. Jesus wasn't criticizing action; He was honoring attention. In a culture that often equates worth with doing, the Rabbi celebrates being still long enough to hear Him.

Prompt:

- *Where in your life is busyness crowding out presence?*
- *What would it look like to "sit at His feet" this week?*

DAY 2 — A DISCIPLE'S POSTURE

Scripture Readings:

- *Acts 22:3 — Paul "at the feet of Gamaliel"*
- *Psalm 27:4 — "to gaze on the beauty of the Lord"*

Reflection: To sit at a rabbi's feet was a formal declaration of discipleship. It wasn't passive. It was an act of intentional surrender. Paul claimed it. Mary lived it. And the Psalms longed for it. Presence is not idleness. It's formation. It's how disciples are shaped — by the voice of the Rabbi, not just by the mission.

Application Questions:

- *Is your walk with Jesus more focused on movement or on being with Him?*
- *What rhythms might you change to reflect a posture of presence?*

DAY 3 — ECHOES OF THE PATH

Mishnah Insight:

"Not learning, but doing is the main thing."

— AVOT 1:17

Yet Mary reminds us: *Being precedes both.*

Reflection: The disciple's heart is not transactional. We follow not because of what we get, but because of who He is. Faithfulness that costs nothing is often worth just as little.

Prompt:

- *Have I mistaken busyness for spiritual maturity?*
- *When was the last time I listened more than I spoke in prayer?*

DAY 4 — A HEART AT REST

Story:
A young mother once said,

"My soul finally quieted when I realized I didn't have to impress Jesus — just sit with Him."

Discipleship isn't about keeping up. It's about slowing down long enough for the Rabbi's dust to settle on your skin, your thoughts, your calendar. Mary understood what the world rarely applauds: the greatest strength is stillness rooted in love.**Challenge:** Identify something you value that might be **competing with your calling**.

Challenge Questions:

- *What's one way you can reclaim stillness this week?*
- *Where do you need to stop striving and simply be with Jesus?*

DAY 5 — THE COVENANT MIRROR

Reflect with honesty:

1. *Am I more comfortable serving Jesus than sitting with Him?*
2. *What lies do I believe about my worth being tied to activity?*
3. *How might sitting at His feet re-center my identity?*
4. *What do I fear I'll hear if I slow down and really listen?*
5. *Who in my life models a lifestyle of presence more than performance?*

Write what stands out. Sit with the silence. Let the Spirit speak.

DAY 6 — WALK IT OUT

Visible Step: Create intentional space this week to "sit at His feet":

- Choose a chair, a room, or a time where you will be fully still.
- Turn off distractions. Sit in silence. Read just one verse.
- Listen. Don't rush to act. Let His words shape you.

Let your obedience cost you something.

Prayer:

Rabbi Jesus,
I've run so hard I've forgotten to rest. But You invite me to sit — not in guilt, but in grace.
Teach me again to be still, To listen,
To love You with my attention,
And to rise only when You say, "Let's walk."
Amen.

OPTIONAL — SABBATH GATHERING / GROUP QUESTIONS

1. *What does "sitting at His feet" look like in your daily life?*
2. *How have you struggled with performance-based faith?*
3. *What did you learn this week by slowing down and listening?*

WEEK 6: IMITATING THE TEACHER

BASED ON CHAPTER 6 OF DUSTPRINTS OF THE RABBI

Focus Verse:

____

"Everyone who is fully trained will be like their teacher."

— LUKE 6:40

____

Theme: To follow a rabbi was to imitate him in every word, action, and sacrifice. Jesus doesn't just want believers — He calls for imitators.

Week Preview: In Jesus' world, to be a disciple wasn't just to agree — it was to imitate. The highest aim of a Talmid (disciple) was not to know what his rabbi knew, but to live as his rabbi lived. This week, you'll be challenged to ask hard questions about how closely your life mirrors your Teacher's. Do your priorities, relationships, and reactions reflect His? To walk behind Jesus is to become like Him — not in title, but in practice.

DAY 1 — BECOMING LIKE THE RABBI

Scripture: *Luke 6:37–42*

Reflection: Jesus doesn't measure discipleship by belief statements. He measures it by likeness. Mercy, humility, truth-telling, self-examination — these aren't electives for the serious few. They're the core curriculum. To be fully trained under Jesus means that people begin to see Him when they see you.

Prompt:

- *Where do my actions most reflect my Rabbi?*
- *Where do they least reflect Him?*

DAY 2 — FOLLOWING THE DUSTPRINTS

Scripture Readings:

- *1 Peter 2:21–25*
- *John 13:12–17*

Reflection: Jesus didn't just blaze a path — He walked one meant to be followed. He knelt. He forgave. He suffered without retaliation. When Peter later wrote about following in Jesus' steps, it wasn't poetic. It was painful. It meant a cross-shaped life, soaked in grace. You don't have to invent the path — you just have to step into the dustprints already there.

Application Questions:

- *What does it mean for me to "follow His steps" in my home, work, or church?*
- *What's one behavior Jesus is inviting me to imitate more fully?*

DAY 3 — A DISCIPLE'S HALAKHAH

Mishnah Insight:

"Be covered in the dust of your teacher, and drink in his words with thirst."

— PIRKEI AVOT 1:4

Reflection: *Halakhah* — "the way one walks" — was the embodiment of a rabbi's teachings. Jesus didn't just teach ideas. He modeled a way of life: eating with outcasts, speaking with courage, withdrawing in prayer, washing feet. His disciples weren't students — they were apprentices in holiness.

Prompt:

- *If someone watched my life, what would they assume about my Rabbi?*
- *What part of my walk needs to be re-trained by His?*

DAY 4 — THE COST OF IMITATION

Story:

A Christian aid worker in the Middle East was once asked why she stayed despite danger. She replied, "Because my Rabbi didn't run when things got hard. He leaned in." Imitating Jesus doesn't always look like success. Sometimes it looks like sacrifice — like forgiving when you've been wronged or staying when it would be easier to leave.

Challenge Questions:

- *What aspect of Jesus' life feels hardest to imitate?*
- *Where is He inviting you to reflect Him more boldly?*

DAY 5 — THE COVENANT MIRROR

Sit with these questions:

1. *What do I admire about Jesus but still resist becoming like?*
2. *Who in my life has best reflected the likeness of Christ?*
3. *What would imitation cost me right now — comfort, reputation, pride?*
4. *In what area is God asking me to act like Jesus instead of just praying about it?*
5. *Would someone know I'm a follower of Jesus by how I treat the least?*

Write what stands out. Sit with the silence. Let the Spirit speak.

DAY 6 — WALK IT OUT

Visible Challenge: Pick one act this week that mirrors Jesus in a specific way:

- *Forgive someone who didn't ask.*
- *Serve someone without recognition.*
- *Stand for truth when it costs you.*
- *Choose silence when it's easier to lash out*

Prayer:

Rabbi Jesus,
I don't just want to believe in You — I want to be like You.
Train my steps.
Shape my instincts.
Let my life reflect Your dust,
And let others see You in the way I walk.
Amen.

OPTIONAL — SABBATH GATHERING / GROUP QUESTIONS

1. Where did you most imitate Jesus this week?
2. What area of your life still needs to be shaped more by His walk?
3. How can the group support you in becoming more like the Rabbi?

WEEK 7: THE COST OF THE CALL

BASED ON CHAPTER 7 OF DUSTPRINTS OF THE RABBI

Focus Verse:

"Whoever wants to be My disciple must deny themselves and take up their cross daily and follow Me."

— LUKE 9:23

Theme: Discipleship is free — but it will cost you everything. To follow Jesus is to die to self, surrender control, and walk wherever the Rabbi leads.

Week Preview: Jesus never used fine print. When He called disciples, He made the cost clear. This wasn't a casual invitation — it was a covenant summons. In the first-century Jewish world, to follow a rabbi meant leaving behind your old identity, your family's expectations, even your livelihood. It was radical, it was real, and it still is. This week, you'll wrestle with what Jesus' invitation costs you — and why it's worth everything.

DAY 1 — NO TURNING BACK

Scripture: *Luke 9:57–62*

Reflection: Three would-be disciples offered Jesus conditional obedience. Each one wanted to follow, but on their terms. Jesus responded with piercing clarity: *"No one who puts a hand to the plow and looks back is fit for the kingdom."* The call to follow requires forward motion — no backup plan, no second thoughts.

Prompt:

- *What conditions have I placed on my obedience?*
- *What part of my old life do I still glance back toward?*

DAY 2 — TAKE UP YOUR CROSS

Scripture Readings:

- *Luke 14:25–33*
- *Galatians 2:20*

Reflection: Jesus didn't promise comfort. He promised a cross. In His culture, the cross wasn't a metaphor — it was an execution stake. To carry one meant death. And yet, that's the path of the disciple: dying daily to ego, entitlement, and ease, so something greater can live.

Application Questions:

- *What part of me needs to die in order for Christ to live more fully?*
- *Have I confused spiritual growth with spiritual comfort?*

DAY 3 — THE PRICE AND THE PEARL

Mishnah Insight:

"This world is like a vestibule before the world to come; prepare yourself in the vestibule so that you may enter the banquet hall."

— PIRKEI AVOT 4:21

Reflection: Jesus told of a merchant who sold everything to buy a pearl. That's what the Kingdom costs — everything. But it's worth far more. Ancient rabbis taught that life here prepares us for the world to come. Jesus calls us to live like it now — selling lesser things to gain eternal treasure.

Prompt:

- *What am I still clinging to that cannot follow me into the Kingdom?*
- *Where is Jesus asking me to trade comfort for eternal purpose?*

DAY 4 — WHEN THE CALL HURTS

Story:

A young believer left a lucrative career to serve refugees. When asked why, she simply said, "Because He asked." Obedience is rarely easy. The cost is real — reputation, stability, relationships. But the call is clearer still. When you hear it, you either go — or you walk away dustless.

Challenge Questions:

- *What has following Jesus cost you so far?*
- *What cost are you still counting?*

DAY 5 — THE COVENANT MIRROR

Ask honestly:

1. *Where do I hesitate to obey Jesus because it feels too costly?*
2. *What sacrifices have I avoided — and what has it cost me spiritually?*
3. *How does fear of discomfort shape my discipleship choices?*
4. *What might obedience look like in the next 24 hours?*
5. *Do I believe the Kingdom is worth everything?*

Write what stands out. Sit with the silence. Let the Spirit speak.

DAY 6 — WALK IT OUT

Visible Challenge: This week, take one costly step toward deeper discipleship:

- Give up something valuable to serve someone else.
- Apologize or reconcile even if it's uncomfortable.
- Step into a ministry, need, or opportunity you've been resisting.

Prayer:

Jesus,
You carried the cross so I could carry mine.
Teach me to surrender — not because it's easy,
but because You are worthy.
Strip away my conditions.
Call me again.
And I will follow.
Amen.

OPTIONAL — SABBATH GATHERING / GROUP QUESTIONS

1. *What cost challenged you the most this week?*
2. *How has Jesus been more than worth the sacrifice?*
3. *What next step will deepen your obedience?*

WEEK 8: TRUSTING THE DUSTY PATH

BASED ON CHAPTER 8 OF DUSTPRINTS OF THE RABBI

Focus Verse:

"Blessed are those who have not seen and yet have believed."

— JOHN 20:29B

Theme: Sometimes the path behind the Rabbi grows dim, silent, and uncertain — but true disciples keep walking, trusting that His dust still leads.

Week Preview: Faith is not forged in clarity — it's tested in the dust. The ancient paths of discipleship wind through uncertainty, wilderness, and waiting. The Rabbi does not promise full vision — He promises presence. This week, you'll walk the road of faith when the way feels unclear. And you'll discover that even when you can't see where He's leading, the dust still means He's near.

DAY 1 — THE ROAD OF NOT KNOWING

Scripture: *John 20:24–29*

Reflection: Thomas wanted proof. Jesus offered peace. Doubt isn't the opposite of faith — it's a threshold. When the way is dim, we don't need to see the whole road. We just need to trust that the dust still rises ahead of us — and that the Rabbi never walks alone.

Prompt:

- *Where are you waiting for answers before you'll move?*
- *What would it mean to walk forward even without clarity?*

DAY 2 — FAITH IN THE WILDERNESS

Scripture Readings:

- *Exodus 13:17–22*
- *Hebrews 11:8–10*

Reflection: God didn't lead Israel on the shortest route. He led them on the one that would shape them. Abraham followed without knowing where. The wilderness is not a detour — it's the curriculum of trust. It strips away illusions and calls us to follow not with our eyes, but with our hearts.

Application Questions:

- *What part of your story feels like a wilderness?*
- *How might God be forming faith in what feels like delay?*

DAY 3 — ECHOES OF THE PATH

Mishnah Insight:

"Say little and do much."

— *PIRKEI AVOT 1:15*

Reflection: God often works in silence. Between the Red Sea and the Promised Land, there were long stretches of quiet. The Rabbi doesn't always explain His steps — but He never stops walking. Faith means stepping anyway. Trusting the silence. Following the footprints, not the spotlight.

Prompt:

- *When have you mistaken silence for absence?*
- *What do you need to hear from God — and what is He asking you to do while you wait?*

DAY 4 — WHEN THE DUST BLOWS BACK

Story:

A man once said,

"It felt like I was walking through a storm, not a path."

But dust in the wind is still dust — it means someone went ahead of you. Even when it clouds your view, it confirms the Rabbi is still moving. Faith doesn't always feel certain — but it always keeps walking.

Challenge Questions:

- *What's one area of life where you're tempted to stop walking?*
- *Where do you need to trust that the Rabbi is still ahead — even if the dust blinds you?*

DAY 5 — THE COVENANT MIRROR

Examine your heart with these questions:

1. *Where am I waiting for clarity before obeying?*
2. *What wilderness season still lingers in my heart?*
3. *Have I confused God's quietness with His absence?*
4. *How does uncertainty invite me into deeper faith?*
5. *What small step of obedience can I take today, even without answers? mercy — or just accept it when I'm the one in need?*

Write what stands out. Sit with the silence. Let the Spirit speak.

DAY 6 — WALK IT OUT

Visible Challenge: Step forward this week in one area of uncertainty or fear:

- Begin something God has placed on your heart — without all the details.
- Reach out, give, or serve in a way that requires trust, not control.
- Create space for silence — and listen longer than you speak.

Prayer:

Rabbi Jesus,

I cannot always see the road — but I trust Your feet still stir the dust.

Lead me through the silence.

Strengthen my soul in the fog.

And help me walk not by sight, but by faith.

Amen.

OPTIONAL — SABBATH GATHERING / GROUP QUESTIONS

1. *What tested your trust this week?*
2. *Where did you take a step without having full understanding?*
3. *How can your group support each other in walking through silence?*

WEEK 9: FOLLOWING THROUGH THE WILDERNESS

BASED ON CHAPTER 9 OF DUSTPRINTS OF THE RABBI

Focus Verse:

"So He humbled you, allowed you to hunger, and fed you with manna...that He might make you know that man shall not live by bread alone; but man lives by every word that proceeds from the mouth of the LORD."

— DEUTERONOMY 8:3

Theme: The wilderness is not the absence of God's presence — it is the place where trust becomes formation, and the disciple learns to depend on nothing but the voice of the Rabbi.

Week Preview: No one wants the wilderness. But every disciple walks through it. The desert isn't a mistake or a punishment — it's where the deepest transformation happens. This week, we step into the dustier places of the path — the lonely, dry, uncertain moments that stretch our faith and strip us of self-sufficiency. The wilderness teaches what the classroom cannot. And it's where the Rabbi walks closest.

DAY 1 — LED BY THE SPIRIT

Scripture: *Matthew 4:1–4*

Reflection: Jesus was led into the wilderness — not by mistake, but by the Spirit. The same God who parted seas also sends His people into silence. Why? Because hunger teaches dependence. Isolation reveals the idols we carry. And dust becomes the doorway to deeper trust.

Prompt:

- *Where have you resisted the wilderness rather than followed through it?*
- *What does your heart reach for when God feels distant?*

DAY 2 — BREAD FROM HEAVEN

Scripture ReadingS:

- *Exodus 16:1–5*
- *Deuteronomy 8:1–6*

Reflection: Manna came one day at a time. The Israelites couldn't store it or stretch it. They had to trust — daily. Jesus called Himself the Bread of Life, not the Planner of All Things. The wilderness forces you to rely on grace that's fresh each morning — not strategy or strength.

Application Questions:

- *What "manna" is God giving you right now that you're tempted to ignore?*
- *How is He teaching you to live from His voice more than your vision?*

DAY 3 — WALKING IN CIRCLES

Midrash Insight:

"In the desert, the heart listens."

— *MIDRASH TANCHUMA, BAMIDBAR 7*

Reflection: Forty years. That's how long Israel wandered — not because of distance, but because of formation. The wilderness strips away noise, routine, and false identity. It's where the heart begins to hear what it could not hear in Egypt or in Canaan. Don't despise the circles — they're carving trust into your soul.

Prompt:

- *What am I learning in the "unmoving" places?*
- *How is God using repetition to form something deeper in me?*

DAY 4 — STILL FOLLOWING

Story:

A woman battling chronic illness once said, "Even when I

can't feel Him, I picture His dust. That's enough to keep me moving." Some days, following Jesus feels like movement. Other days, it's endurance. But trust isn't proven when the path is clear — it's proven when your feet are blistered and you keep walking anyway.

Challenge Questions:

- *What's one way you can keep walking this week — even without answers?*
- *How does faith look different in the wilderness than in blessing?*

DAY 5 — THE COVENANT MIRROR

Ask honestly:

1. *What wilderness have I tried to escape instead of endure?*
2. *Where have I seen God provide daily when I wanted a plan?*
3. *Am I willing to trust God's voice more than my preferences?*
4. *What spiritual hunger is the wilderness awakening in me?*
5. *What kind of disciple is this dry season forming in me?*

Write what stands out. Sit with the silence. Let the Spirit speak.

DAY 6 — WALK IT OUT

Visible Challenge: Embrace the wilderness this week in a visible way:

- Share your story of wilderness with someone who feels alone.
- Fast from something that numbs your spiritual hunger.
- Memorize Deuteronomy 8:3 — and pray it aloud in moments of dryness

Prayer:

Rabbi Jesus,
You walked into the wilderness first.
You know the heat. The silence. The thirst.
Teach me to follow, even when the path feels dry.
Let manna come again.
Let Your Word sustain me.
And let the wilderness become holy ground.
Amen.

OPTIONAL — SABBATH GATHERING / GROUP QUESTIONS

1. *How have you experienced the wilderness in this season?*
2. *What has God revealed about Himself in your wilderness?*
3. *How can you support one another as you walk through dustier parts of the path?*

WEEK 10: THE JOURNEY TO JERUSALEM

BASED ON CHAPTER 10 OF DUSTPRINTS OF THE RABBI

Focus Verse:

"As the time approached for Him to be taken up to heaven, Jesus resolutely set out for Jerusalem"

— LUKE 9:51

Theme: Every disciple must one day follow the Rabbi to Jerusalem — the place of calling, surrender, sacrifice, and glory.

Week Preview: Jesus didn't avoid Jerusalem. He set His face toward it. He knew the suffering waiting there — and still, He walked. Discipleship always moves toward surrender. For Jesus, Jerusalem was the place where obedience met agony. This week invites you to examine where your own road leads — and to follow the Rabbi, even when the destination is costly.

DAY 1 — SET YOUR FACE

Scripture: *Luke 9:51–56*

Reflection: Jesus knew what Jerusalem meant — betrayal, beating, crucifixion. Still, He "set His face" toward it. In Hebraic thought, this phrase reflects immovable resolve. To walk behind the Rabbi means that eventually, your feet trace His path to surrender. And you don't hesitate — you set your face too.

Prompt:

- *Where in your life is Jesus asking you to stop delaying and start walking?*
- *What would it look like to say "yes" with resolve?*

DAY 2 — THE CITY OF DECISION

Scripture Readings:

- *Psalm 122:1–4*
- *John 12:12–26*

Reflection: For centuries, pilgrims went "up to Jerusalem" to worship, to sacrifice, to meet with God. Jesus entered not just as a pilgrim — but as the Lamb. The journey to Jerusalem is always layered: hope, fear, devotion, surrender. It's not a place on a map — it's a crossroads of the soul.

Application Questions:

- *What "Jerusalem" moment is God leading you toward right now?*
- *Are you trying to delay a sacrifice that actually leads to glory?*

DAY 3 — THE PATH OF THE LAMB

Midrash Insight:

"When a man sacrifices something of his own, it is as if he offered himself."

— MIDRASH VAYIKRA RABBAH 2:5

Reflection: To the Jewish mind, sacrifice wasn't simply about offering an animal — it was about offering yourself through it. Jesus did not just teach this — He became it. The disciple's path to Jerusalem is never symbolic. It is deeply personal. When we surrender our comfort, pride, or safety, we walk in the Rabbi's shadow.

Prompt:

- *What part of your life is God asking you to place on the altar?*
- *How is surrender becoming more than theory?*

DAY 4 — A DIFFERENT KIND OF GLORY

Story:

A young leader left behind public recognition for a quieter role that aligned with calling but not applause. "The Lord asked me to go to my Jerusalem," she said. "It looked like dying, but it turned out to be life." The road to Jerusalem is always the road to deeper obedience. And resurrection only comes after surrender.

Challenge Questions:

- *What step of obedience feels like crucifixion — but might lead to resurrection?*
- *How has God used past surrenders to birth new life?*

DAY 5 — THE COVENANT MIRROR

Reflect deeply:

1. *What "Jerusalem" do I fear walking toward right now?*
2. *Have I mistaken comfort for calling?*
3. *Where have I delayed obedience out of fear of what it will cost?*
4. *What would it mean to set my face like flint and walk forward?*
5. *Who is watching my journey — and learning what faith looks like?*

Write what stands out. Sit with the silence. Let the Spirit speak.

DAY 6 — WALK IT OUT

Visible Challenge: This week, walk boldly toward what you've been resisting:

- Have a hard conversation.
- Step into a calling you've delayed.
- Fast, pray, or give sacrificially — not to earn approval, but to express surrender.

Prayer:

Rabbi Jesus,
You did not turn back.
You walked to Jerusalem with dust on Your feet and surrender in Your heart.
Teach me to walk with that kind of courage.
Let obedience lead me where glory lives.
And let my steps trace Yours — all the way home.
Amen.

OPTIONAL — SABBATH GATHERING / GROUP QUESTIONS

1. *What "Jerusalem" are you currently facing — and how is God meeting you there?*
2. *Where have you seen obedience lead to unexpected grace?*
3. *What encouragement do you need to take the next faithful step?*

WEEK 11: THE HIDDEN STRENGTH (MEEKNESS)

BASED ON CHAPTER 11 OF DUSTPRINTS OF THE RABBI

Focus Verse:

"Blessed are the meek, for they shall inherit the earth."

— MATTHEW 5:5

Theme: Meekness is not weakness. In the Kingdom of God, true strength is found in surrender — in the quiet power of a life yielded to the Rabbi's voice.

Week Preview: In the Greco-Roman world, power came through dominance. But Jesus taught that strength was revealed in restraint. Meekness, in the Hebraic sense, is not passivity — it is focused humility, a strength under the control of the Spirit. This week, you'll learn how to walk in the power of quiet obedience, trusting that those who seem overlooked by the world may be those God trusts to carry His inheritance.

DAY 1 — THE STRENGTH YOU DON'T SEE

Scripture: *Matthew 5:1–12*

Reflection: Jesus opened His most famous teaching by honoring the lowly. The meek. The mourners. The hungry. He flipped every definition of strength. Meekness is not being voiceless — it's knowing when not to raise your voice. It's power restrained by love. And according to Jesus, it's the way to *inherit the earth*.

Prompt:

- *Where am I confusing volume with influence?*
- *How could I reflect strength through restraint this week?*

DAY 2 — A GENTLE MESSIAH

Scripture Readings:

- *Isaiah 42:1–4*
- *Matthew 11:28–30*

Reflection: Jesus fulfilled the prophecy of a Servant who would not break a bruised reed. He carried power that could have crushed — but He chose to restore. His yoke is gentle, His strength never self-serving. Meekness is not shrinking back — it is moving forward without needing to control.

Application Questions:

- *What does it look like to walk gently in my relationships this week?*

- *What is one area where I'm tempted to force instead of follow?*

DAY 3 — INHERITING THE EARTH

Mishnah Insight:

"One who is humble and fears sin will not lose his place in the world to come.

— AVOT 6:6

Reflection: Humility, in Jewish teaching, was tied to wisdom and divine favor. The one who walks humbly before God doesn't lose — they are lifted. When Jesus said the meek would "inherit the earth," He wasn't offering poetic comfort — He was making a covenant promise: the Kingdom belongs to the quietly faithful.

Prompt:

- *Where am I striving for control that God has already promised to provide?*
- *How does humility make room for greater peace?*

DAY 4 — POWER UNDER CONTROL

Story:

A respected elder once said nothing in a heated argument. When asked why, he replied, "I trust the Spirit to speak louder than I can." That is meekness. It doesn't retreat — it resists reacting. In a culture obsessed with being seen and heard, meekness remembers: the Rabbi sees. And He will reward.

Challenge Questions:

- *Where is God calling you to choose restraint over reaction?*
- *What does it look like to trust that unseen strength still bears fruit?*

DAY 5 — THE COVENANT MIRROR

Ask with courage:

1. *When have I confused meekness with weakness?*
2. *Where have I misused strength — even subtly — to get my way?*
3. *Who in my life reflects the meekness of Jesus?*
4. *What would change if I believed the meek will truly inherit the earth?*
5. *What's one step toward quieter, Spirit-led strength I can take this week?*

Write what stands out. Sit with the silence. Let the Spirit speak.

DAY 6 — WALK IT OUT

Visible Challenge: Practice quiet strength this week:

- *Remain silent when provoked — and pray instead.*

- *Let go of one "control point" in your life and surrender it.*
- *Encourage someone privately who rarely receives affirmation.*

Prayer:

Rabbi Jesus,
You didn't shout to prove Your power.
You walked in quiet authority.
Teach me the courage of the meek.
Train me to trust the strength of surrender.
Let me walk softly — but with purpose.
And lead me to the inheritance only You can give.
Amen.

OPTIONAL — SABBATH GATHERING / GROUP QUESTIONS

1. *What surprised you about the nature of meekness this week?*
2. *How have you seen Jesus model strength through surrender?*
3. *What area of your life do you need to release to the Spirit's control?*

WEEK 12: RABBI OF THE CROSS

BASED ON CHAPTER 12 OF DUSTPRINTS OF THE RABBI

Focus Verse:

"Whoever wants to be My disciple must deny themselves and take up their cross and follow Me."

— LUKE 9:23

Theme: The Rabbi we follow does not just teach from a scroll — He leads to a cross. True discipleship embraces suffering, surrender, and the paradox of a crucified King.

Week Preview: Discipleship doesn't stop at the mount of miracles. It walks with the Rabbi to the place of execution. In Jesus' world, the cross was not a metaphor. It was Rome's declaration of shame, power, and finality. But Jesus turned it into the doorway of the Kingdom. This week, we follow a Rabbi who does not avoid the cross — He embraces it. And He calls us to do the same.

DAY 1 — THE PATH TO GOLGOTHA

Scripture: *Luke 23:26–33*

Reflection: The road to Golgotha was soaked in pain, dust, and silence. Jesus carried the crossbeam while the crowd mocked and mourned. To follow Him means stepping into places that are not triumphant — but sacrificial. Real discipleship gets bloody. And holy.

Prompt:

- Where is Jesus calling you to follow Him — not in glory, but in grief?
- How does the cross reshape your expectations of what faith looks like?

DAY 2 — MOCKED, NOT MISSED

Scripture Readings:

- *Isaiah 53:1–7*
- *Hebrews 12:1–3*

Reflection: He was "despised and rejected." Not because He failed — but because He surrendered. The cross is a confrontation: of pride, of power, of comfort. The joy set before Jesus wasn't ease. It was resurrection. But first, He endured. So must we.

Application Questions:

- *Where am I resisting endurance because I want ease?*
- *What joy might be waiting on the other side of my surrender?*

DAY 3 — THE DEATH OF SELF

Talmud Insight:

"When one humbles himself, the Holy One raises him up."

— TAANIT 7A

Reflection: The Talmud teaches that humility precedes elevation. Jesus didn't die because He was weak — He died because He was obedient. The cross wasn't a collapse — it was a coronation. Every time you choose humility, you echo the cross. And the Rabbi smiles.

Prompt:

- *What area of your life is dying right now — and how might that be part of your rising?*
- *Where can you embrace humility instead of defending yourself?*

DAY 4 — HE CARRIED IT FIRST

Midrash Insight:

"God does not assign suffering to His people without first bearing it Himself."

— MIDRASH TEHILLIM 91

Story:

A father watching his son suffer said,

"I would carry it if I could."

At the cross, God did. He didn't watch from heaven — He entered the suffering. The Rabbi of the Cross didn't just teach about pain. He bled. And He still walks with you through yours.

Challenge Questions:

- *What part of your pain do you need to let Jesus carry with you?*
- *How does it change your view of God to know He suffers with you?*

DAY 5 — THE COVENANT MIRROR

Ask with honesty:

1. *Where have I expected resurrection without crucifixion?*

2. *What comforts or entitlements do I struggle to release?*
3. *How have I seen Jesus walk with me in my own suffering?*
4. *Where am I called to walk in quiet sacrifice this week?*
5. *What part of me still resists the cross — and what might be waiting if I surrender?*

Write what stands out. Sit with the silence. Let the Spirit speak.

DAY 6 — WALK IT OUT

Visible Challenge: Embrace cross-shaped obedience this week:

- Forgive someone who doesn't deserve it.
- Sacrifice a comfort to make room for someone else's healing.
- Serve in a place where no one sees or applauds.

Prayer:
Rabbi Jesus,
You didn't just teach the Word — You carried the cross.
You didn't just speak truth — You lived it through suffering.
Teach me not to run from the hard path.
Help me walk behind You,
Even to Golgotha,
Until resurrection breaks forth again.
Amen.

OPTIONAL — SABBATH GATHERING / GROUP QUESTIONS

1. *Where have you encountered the cross this week — personally or spiritually?*
2. *What changed when you surrendered instead of fought?*
3. *How can your group support one another in carrying what Jesus asks of you?*

WEEK 13: BEARING THE RABBI'S AUTHORITY

BASED ON CHAPTER 13 OF DUSTPRINTS OF THE RABBI

Focus Verse:

"All authority in heaven and on earth has been given to Me. Therefore go..."

— MATTHEW 28:18–19A

Theme: The authority of the Rabbi is not for status — it's for service. Jesus entrusts His authority to those who walk in His dust, live in His ways, and carry His Name with humility.

Week Preview: In Jesus' world, only a rabbi with *s'mikhah* — divine authority — could give new interpretations of Torah and commission others to carry on his teachings. When Jesus said, "All authority has been given to Me," He wasn't just declaring power — He was inviting disciples to share in His mission. This week explores what it means to bear the

Rabbi's authority: to live with heaven's endorsement, not for personal glory, but for global transformation.

DAY 1 — THE WEIGHT OF HIS WORDS

Scripture: *Matthew 28:16–20*

Reflection: Jesus didn't just rise — He commissioned. After conquering death, He passed on His authority to flawed followers. That authority isn't permission to control. It's power to represent. To speak His words. To live His truth. When you bear the Rabbi's authority, your life echoes His voice.

Prompt:

- *Where am I being called to speak or act on behalf of the Kingdom?*
- *How do I represent Jesus in my home, work, and relationships?*

DAY 2 —WALKING IN THE NAME

Scripture Readings:

- *Acts 3:1–10 — Peter and John heal the lame man*
- *John 14:12–14 — "In My name..."*

Reflection: Peter didn't say, "Look at me." He said, "In the name of Jesus…walk." Authority in the ancient world meant representation — acting under someone's name. Jesus gives you His name. That means your prayers carry His boldness, your obedience carries His signature, and your compassion carries His touch.

Application Questions:

- *Where have I forgotten the power of Jesus' name in everyday life?*
- *How does spiritual authority look different from human influence?*

DAY 3 — FROM STUDENT TO STEWARD

Mishnah Insight:

"Be deliberate in judgment, raise up many disciples, and make a fence around the Torah."

— PIRKEI AVOT 1:1

Reflection: The early rabbis passed on authority carefully. They raised up disciples who would guard, transmit, and embody their teaching. Jesus does the same — but with a revolutionary twist: He sends us out to the nations, empowered not to protect rules, but to bring life. You are not just a student — you are a steward of the Kingdom.

Prompt:

- *What teaching or truth has Jesus entrusted to you to carry and share?*
- *Are you guarding it with reverence or hiding it in fear?*

DAY 4 —AUTHORITY THAT WASHES FEET

Talmud Insight:

"Where there is humility, there is greatness."

— SOTAH 5A

Story:

A young pastor was once asked what authority looked like. He walked over, picked up a towel, and began to wash someone's feet. "This," he said. That's the Jesus-model. His authority didn't come with robes and scrolls — it came with scars and servanthood. The greatest authority in the Kingdom is given to the lowest servant.

Challenge Questions:

- *Where is Jesus asking you to step down so He can raise you up?*
- *How can your leadership — in any context — become more like His?*

DAY 5 — THE COVENANT MIRROR

Reflect with clarity:

1. *Where have I confused spiritual authority with human power?*
2. *How has God entrusted me to carry His message or presence?*

3. *Do I walk with confidence in His name — or hesitation?*
4. *Where is He calling me to represent Him more boldly or compassionately?*
5. *What does it look like to lead like Jesus — in my unique setting?*

Write what stands out. Sit with the silence. Let the Spirit speak.

DAY 6 — WALK IT OUT

Visible Challenge: Exercise spiritual authority this week in tangible, humble ways:

- Pray boldly for someone who needs healing, hope, or direction.
- Speak Jesus' name into a conversation that needs light.
- Serve someone in secret as an act of Christlike leadership.

Prayer:
Jesus,
You have all authority — and You entrust it to those who follow You.
Teach me to carry it humbly,
To speak only what You say,
And to walk only where You lead.
Let my life bear Your name with holiness.
Amen.

OPTIONAL — SABBATH GATHERING / GROUP QUESTIONS

1. *What does it mean to you to bear the Rabbi's authority?*
2. *How have you seen Jesus' name bring transformation in your life or others'?*
3. *Where do you feel challenged to lead more like Jesus this week?*

WEEK 14: A LEGACY OF DUSTPRINTS

BASED ON CHAPTER 14 OF DUSTPRINTS OF THE RABBI

Focus Verse:

"Follow my example, as I follow the example of Christ."

— 1 CORINTHIANS 11:1

Theme: The disciple's life was never meant to end with personal growth. True discipleship leaves a trail. You were not just called to walk in the dust — you were called to leave some behind for others to follow.

Week Preview: Every step behind the Rabbi is a step someone else might follow. That's the nature of discipleship. It's not only about being formed — it's about forming others. This week calls you to think beyond your journey and begin to live a life that points to Jesus long after you're gone. Dustprint by dustprint, the path of the Kingdom continues.

DAY 1 — FOLLOW ME AS I FOLLOW

SCRIPTURES:

- *1 Corinthians 11:1*
- *Philippians 3:17*

Reflection: Paul wasn't arrogant when he said, "Follow me." He was accountable. He understood that discipleship always leaves footprints. If you're walking behind the Rabbi, your dust is falling on someone else's shoes — a friend, a child, a neighbor. That's not pressure. That's purpose.

Prompt:

- *Who is already watching how you walk?*
- *What parts of your life reflect the Rabbi's rhythm — and which don't?*

DAY 2 — DUST GENERATIONS

Scripture Readings:

- *Deuteronomy 6:4–9*
- *2 Timothy 2:2*

Reflection: The Shema called Israel to pass down their walk to the next generation — not with slogans, but with lifestyle. Paul charged Timothy to do the same. Discipleship is not just what you believe. It's what you repeat. What you embody. What you leave behind.

Application Questions:

- *What legacy of faith are you actively forming right now?*
- *What do others learn about Jesus from your habits, schedule, and speech?*

DAY 3 — A TRAIL WORTH FOLLOWING

Midrash Insight:

"The righteous leave behind not silver or gold, but deeds which shine like the firmament."

— MIDRASH TEHILLIM 112

Reflection: In Hebraic tradition, legacy was not measured in wealth, but in witness. The greatest inheritance is a life that radiates the holiness of God. Every unseen act of obedience, every quiet sacrifice, every step in the Rabbi's dust becomes a signpost for the next disciple.

Prompt:

- *Am I investing more in what will outlive me or what will outshine me?*
- *What "deeds" do I want to leave behind?*

DAY 4 —WHAT WILL THEY REMEMBER?

Talmud Insight:

"A person is remembered not for what they had, but for how they walked."

— BERAKHOT 17A

Story:
An old rabbi once said,

"I want my grandchildren to remember not my sermons, but my prayers."

You don't need a platform to leave a legacy. You just need dust on your feet and Jesus in your steps.
Challenge Questions:

- *What one habit or value do I hope others imitate from my life?*
- *Who do I need to intentionally disciple or invest in?*

DAY 5 — THE COVENANT MIRROR

Ask deeply:

1. What have I been building that will not last beyond me?
2. Who is following me — and am I leading them to Jesus or somewhere else?
3. What part of my life is most "imitable" right now?

4. What do I want people to remember when they talk about how I followed Jesus?
5. What dustprint am I leaving behind in this season?

Write what stands out. Sit with the silence. Let the Spirit speak.

DAY 6 — WALK IT OUT

Visible Challenge: This week, live your legacy — don't just plan for it:

- Have a spiritual conversation with someone younger in the faith.
- Write a letter, prayer, or blessing to the next generation.
- Let your calendar reflect the Kingdom today — not someday.

Prayer:
Rabbi Jesus,
You left a path we could follow.
Now help me do the same.
Let my words, my steps, and my silence point to You.
Let the dust of my walk stir hunger in those who follow.
And let my life leave a trail worth tracing.
Amen.

OPTIONAL — SABBATH GATHERING / GROUP QUESTIONS

1. *What kind of legacy are you currently building?*
2. *Who do you feel called to intentionally disciple or invest in?*
3. *What kind of dustprint do you want to leave in your family, church, or community?*

FINAL REFLECTION: STILL IN THE DUST

THE JOURNEY DOESN'T END. IT DEEPENS.

"Then Jesus said to them again, 'Peace be with you. As the Father has sent Me, I also send you.'"

— JOHN 20:21

CLOSING MEDITATION

You've walked behind the Rabbi for fourteen weeks. Through calling, surrender, silence, strength, and sacrifice. You've traced His steps across ancient paths, and hopefully, through the quiet places of your own life. But this journey doesn't end here.

The dust you carry now is not just His — it's yours. Because wherever you go next, you are now the one leaving dustprints. Not just a follower, but a guide. Not just a student, but a witness.

Discipleship was never just about your formation. It was always about the *sending*. You walk into your home. Your work. Your community. Your conflict. Your worship. And there — in the ordinary — you keep walking in His name.

MIDRASH INSIGHT (FINAL REFLECTION)

"The righteous are like living scrolls — they walk, and the words of God go with them."

— MIDRASH TEHILLIM 119

Let that be your story.
Not that you memorized every page.
But that you walked every day
with the scroll etched into your soul.

REFLECTION QUESTIONS

1. *How has your view of discipleship changed during this journey?*
2. *What one truth from these fourteen weeks do you never want to forget?*
3. *Where is the Spirit calling you to continue this path — and who might follow your dustprints?*

COMMISSIONING PRAYER

Rabbi Jesus,
You invited me to follow —
even when I didn't know where the road would lead.
Now I rise with dust on my feet and fire in my bones.

Send me,
Form me,
Walk with me.
Let my journey leave a trail that leads others to You.
Amen.

APPENDIX: SUGGESTED NEXT STEPS

CONTINUING THE JOURNEY ON THE COVENANT PATH™

You've walked behind the Rabbi for 14 weeks. But this is only the beginning. The Covenant Path is not a curriculum — it's a lifelong journey. Below are suggested next steps to help you continue walking in the dust.

1. **Rewalk the Journey:** Don't hesitate to revisit this devotional. Choose a week that challenged you or revealed something new — and walk it again. His dust never settles the same way twice.
2. **Start a Group:** If you've walked this journey alone, consider inviting 2–4 others to walk with you. Use the *Sabbath Gathering Questions* each week to guide discussion. Discipleship grows deeper in community.
3. **Begin the Next Book:** *Walking in the Dust* is only the beginning. Continue your journey with the next volume in *The Covenant Path ™* series — each one deepening your understanding of Hebraic faith, covenant life, and Jesus-centered discipleship.

4. **Practice Sabbath Rhythms:** Build a weekly Sabbath rhythm into your life:
   - Choose one day to disconnect and delight in God.
   - Reflect on where you followed the Rabbi that week.
   - Light a candle, read a Psalm, bless your family, or walk in quietness.
5. **Pass It On:** Disciples make disciples.
   - Share your devotional with a friend.
   - Write your own "Dustprint Letter" — a testimony or blessing to someone younger in the faith.
   - Ask someone: *"Would you walk with me for the next 14 weeks?"*
6. **Explore the Leader Guide:** Ready to lead others? The companion guide, *Guiding in the Dust*, equips you with everything you need to facilitate groups, walk others through weekly sessions, and create sacred space for others to hear the call of the Rabbi.
7. **Keep Listening:** The dust may settle, but the call never fades.
   - Make space each week to ask: *"Rabbi Jesus, where are You walking today? And may I walk with You."*